FRIENDSHIP

Publisher, Patricia A. Pingry
Executive Editor, Cynthia Wyatt
Art Director, Patrick McRae
Production Manager, Jeff Wyatt
Editorial Assistant, Kathleen Gilbert
Copy Editors, Marian Hollyday
                 Rhonda Colburn

ISBN 0-8249-1076-1

IDEALS—Vol. 46, No. 6 September 1989 IDEALS (ISSN0019-137X) is published eight times a year: February, March, May, June, August, September, November, December by IDEALS PUBLISHING CORPORATION, Nelson Place at Elm Hill Pike, Nashville, Tenn. 37214. Second class postage paid at Nashville, Tennessee, and additional mailing offices. Copyright © 1989 by IDEALS PUBLISHING CORPORATION. POSTMASTER: Send address changes to Ideals, Post Office Box 148000, Nashville, Tenn. 37214-8000. All rights reserved. Title IDEALS registered U.S. Patent Office.

SINGLE ISSUE—$3.95
ONE-YEAR SUBSCRIPTION—eight consecutive issues as published—$17.95
TWO-YEAR SUBSCRIPTION—sixteen consecutive issues as published—$31.95
Outside U.S.A., add $6.00 per subscription year for postage and handling.

The cover and entire contents of IDEALS are fully protected by copyright and must not be reproduced in any manner whatsoever. Printed and bound in U.S.A.

ACKNOWLEDGMENTS

Quotation by Jane Addams from *THE SPIRIT OF YOUTH IN THE CITY STREETS,* Copyright 1909 by Macmillan Publishing; FATHER THUMPS ON THE FLOOR, Copyright 1933, 1935 by Clarence Day and renewed 1963 by Katherine B. Day. Reprinted from *LIFE WITH FATHER* by Clarence Day, by permission of Alfred A. Knopf, Inc.; THE OLD ARMCHAIR from *THROUGH TINTED PANES,* Copyright 1964 by Angela Gall and SEASON TURNABOUT from *REASSURANCE,* Copyright 1988 by Angela Gall. All rights reserved; DISHES from *LIVING THE YEARS* by Edgar A. Guest, Copyright 1949 by The Reilly & Lee Co. Reprinted by permission; THE WHISTLING SWANS by Daniel Whitehead Hicky from *NEVER THE NIGHTINGALE,* Copyright © 1951 by *The New York Times Company.* Reprinted by permission; WE PLAYED TOGETHER from *AUNT HATTIE'S PLACE* by Edna Jaques, Copyright 1941 by Thomas Allen, Ltd. CANADA. Reprinted by permission; THIS I PLEDGE from *AN OLD COPPER DIPPER* by Fannie Dee Robinette Pringle, Copyright 1963. Reprinted by permission; OCTOBER THIRTY-FIRST from *AN OLD CRACKED CUP* by Margaret Curry Rorke, Copyright © 1980 by Northwood Institute Press, Midland, MI. Reprinted by permission; SEPTEMBER IS from *MOMENTS OF SUNSHINE,* Copyright © 1974 by Garnett Ann Shultz. Reprinted by permission; excerpt by Gladys Taber from *THE STILLMEADOW ROAD,* Copyright © 1962 by Gladys Taber. Reprinted by permission of Brandt & Brandt Literary Agents, Inc.; excerpt by Era Zistel from *GENTLE PEOPLE,* Copyright © 1988 by Era Zistel. Published by J.N. Townsend Publishing, Exeter, NH. Reprinted by permission of the Publisher. Our sincere thanks to the following whose addresses we were unable to locate: Marian F. Daggett for FLOWER CALENDAR; M.B. Harrington for PRECIOUS GIFTS; Hanne Redwine for POEM OF FAREWELL TO SUMMER; Fred Toothaker for THE FISHERMEN and ROADSIDE STAND.

Typesetting by The Font Shop, Nashville, Tennessee

Four-color separations by Rayson Films, Inc., Waukesha, Wisconsin

Printing by W.A. Krueger Company, Brookfield, Wisconsin

The paper used in this publication meets the minimum requirements of American National Standard for Information Sciences—Permanence of Paper for Printed Library Materials, ANSI Z39.48-1984.

Front and back covers   Photo Opposite
FLOWERS AND COFFEE   THE GARDEN
Fred Sieb Photography   Gottleib Hampfler

Vol. 46, No. 6

A Southern Garden

Sarah A. Heinzerling

The Adam's needle, slim and straight,
Keeps constant guard down by the gate,
While well-trimmed box in primmest rows
Mark where the gravelled pathway goes.

The hyacinths and violets fling
Their fragrance far in early spring;
The queenly rose through storm and sun,
Month after month blooms grandly on.

Hydrangeas droop their heavy heads
Above the radiant flower beds
Where many gorgeous hues combine
To make a spot with beauty shine.

The heliotrope—the dahlia too—
The pale plumbagoes, heavenly blue,
And even sunflowers, all find room
In season due to grow and bloom.

Before the spruce tree's bristling green,
Some pure white lilies nod and lean
With stately grace each dainty cup
From which the bees delight to sup.

Upon an old tree, shining rings
Of fadeless ivy climb and cling
To form a mantle that will hide
The forest monarch's fallen pride.

And so, in life, true friendship tries
To cover from the cold world's eyes
With charity the faults we find
Within the hearts of humankind.

Photo Opposite
GARDEN
G. Hampfler/H. Armstrong Roberts

THE WHISTLING SWANS

Daniel Whitehead Hicky

For seasons I had waited for this thing,
The whistling swans to seek my marsh again—
When suddenly, out of darkness, wing to wing,
I heard their wild white flutter swift and plain,
Lighting upon the waters where stars were sleeping.
I pushed my door into the trembling night
And sought the marshes' edges, softly creeping
Like a slow secret in the pale moonlight.
Safe in the marsh they floated, spreading wide
Their wings like day unfolding in the sky;
And as I listened as near as I could hide,
I prayed some latening neighbor might happen by
To share that music, far too much for one
To listen to, deep in the night alone.

Photo Opposite
SWANS
H.G. Ross/H. Armstrong Roberts

September Is

Garnett Ann Schultz

September is when crickets chirp
And goldenrod's in bloom;
It's harvesttime and pumpkin pie,
A shining autumn moon.
It's gathering the orchard's fruit—
The treasures of the fall;
And yet midst all the glory,
We hear the winter's call.

September is nostalgia;
It's maples turning gold,
The sumacs' change to brightest red,
The oak so stern and bold.
It's cornshocks in the meadow there;
A richer, bluer sky;
The russet grass and gentle wind;
A tender lullaby.

It's youngsters off to school again
Just at the summer's end,
The cooler air and hazy sun
That autumn days do lend,
A fireplace bright when darkness falls,
The song of katydids,
Fulfillment of our summer dreams—
'Tis this September is.

When It Is September

Garnett Ann Schultz

When it is September, then summer has gone
Along with vacations and games on the lawn;
The children are back in the classrooms once more,
While late flowers of August still bloom by our door.

When it is September, the world sparkles bright
With cool frosty mornings at dawning's first light.
The orchards are golden—there are grapes on the vine,
And sunshine adds beauty to your world and mine.

The sweet smell of autumn adds bright, glowing charms,
While blue skies are gentle above country farms;
There's raking and burning as leaves mount up high,
And mountains reach upward, caressing the sky.

The darkness comes early; the harvesttime's here.
Our families are closer, and dreams are more dear
As quietly, surely, the summer slips by.
When it is September, the world seems to sigh.

MUSHROOMS
David Davis

Invitation
to a
New Friend ©

Carol Bessent Hayman

Knock quietly for entrance to my heart.
The years have left a weather-beaten door;
The latch is a bit stubborn, the frame tight,
But I have kept the glass panes clear and bright.
And once inside, a fire is burning near
Two cosy chairs, a handy stool, and books.
I'll make some tea in Mama's blue teacups,
With homemade bread and butter to serve up.
No need to storm or rush or make a show;
Knock quietly, my friend; my heart will know.

Photo Overleaf
LAST SUMMER HAYFIELD
NEAR SEQUIM, WASHINGTON
Tom Algire

Photo Opposite
INVITING REPAST
Fred Sieb Photography

COUNTRY SUNSHINE

Carol McCrite

Kitchen filled with daisies brought in from a nearby field;
Sweet smell of homegrown peaches freshly picked and carefully peeled;
Squash piled high on a countertop, made ready for a meal;
Country sunshine placed in jars and quickly sealed.

Cantaloupes and melons stacked on the porch in an oval ring;
Tiny, drying peppers hung in rows by coarse brown string;
Butter beans and okra; corn on a summer fling;
Country sunshine's bounty makes me sing.

Hot, steamy smells float out the door in a clearing haze;
Packages ready for the freezer lie heavy on their trays;
Rows of jars line the table and floor in a crazy maze;
Country sunshine stored for winter days.

Photo Opposite
BASKET OF CHEER
H. Armstrong Roberts

First Day of School

Everyone's up early,
Brushing teeth and combing hair,
Packing lunches, eating breakfast—
There's excitement in the air.
Wave good-bye to Mama,
Looking anything but cool.
Nothing's ever so exciting
As that first day of school.

Gladys Clark Fulkerson
Streator, Illinois

October

Brightly shines the sun
    over golden trees.
Darkly gather storm clouds
    over emerald seas.
I sit and let the gentle winds
    blow through my hair,
And breathe deep the changes
    stirring in the autumn air.

Noreen Manfredi
Milltown, New Jersey

Poem of Farewell to Summer

Good-bye to summer!
Good-bye to the sun!
Good-bye to the clouds of weightless cotton above,
Delicious scents,
The softer scent of rainy air.
Good-bye to picnics!
Good-bye to young figures in swimsuits,
Swimming holes,
Suntan lotion's scent.
Good-bye summer. I loved you.

Hanne Redwine
Greenburg, Pennsylvania

A Child's Eyes

Mommy, look! A fairy light
I've caught within my hand.
Oh, a pretty little seed
Blowing across the land.

Mommy, look! I think I found
A rock that's made of gold.
My child, it's what they call "fools,"
And worthless, I've been told.

Mommy, look! A castle strong
Where little elves can play.
But, my child, it's made of sand—
It will quickly wash away.

Mommy, look! The leaves, they dance!
For God alone they twirl.
Yes, my child, I think you're right,
For your heart sees the world.

Laura Barmore
Morgan Hill, California

Reflections

Angels Unaware

It was a rainy night in New Orleans;
At a bus station in the town,
I watched a young girl weeping
As her baggage was taken down.
It seems she'd lost her ticket
Changing buses in the night.
She begged them not to leave her there
With no sign of help in sight.

The bus driver had a face of stone
And his heart was surely the same.
"Losing your ticket's like losing cash money,"
He said and left her in the rain.
Then an old Indian man stood up
And blocked the driver's way
And would not let him pass before
He said what he had to say.
"How can you leave that girl out there?
Have you no God to fear?
You know she had a ticket.
You can't just leave her here.
You can't put her out in a city
Where she doesn't have a friend.
You will meet your schedule,
But she might meet her end."
The driver showed no sign
That he heard or even cared
About the young girl's problem
Or how her travels fared.

So the old Indian gentleman said,
"For her fare I'll pay.
I'll give a little money
To help her on her way."
He went and bought the ticket
And helped her to her place
And helped her put her baggage
In the overhead luggage space.
"How can I repay," she said,
"The kindness you've shown tonight?
We're strangers who won't meet again;
A mere 'thank you' doesn't seem right."

He said, "What goes around comes around.
This I've learned with time—
What you give, you always get back;
What you sow, you reap in kind.
Always be helpful to others
And give what you can spare;
For by being kind to strangers,
We help angels unaware.

Jamie Homer
Nederland, Texas

Editor's Note: Readers are invited to submit unpublished, original poetry, short anecdotes, and humorous reflections on life for possible publication in future *Ideals* issues. Please send copies only; manuscripts will not be returned. Writers receive $10 for each published submission. Send material to "Readers' Reflections," Ideals Publishing Corporation, P.O. Box 140300, Nashville, Tennessee 37214-0300.

Gifts from Friendship's Kitchen

Gifts from the kitchen convey the message of friendship in a special way. These delicious spreads are always appreciated when presented with an assortment of crackers or fruit. The nicest thing about these gifts is that they are meant to be shared with friends and family.

Smoked Salmon Spread

¼ pound smoked salmon, Lox or Nova Scotia, chopped
1 8-ounce package cream cheese, softened
1 tablespoon mayonnaise *or* sour cream
1 green onion, snipped

Blend together all ingredients. Spread on plain or toasted bread rounds or on bagels.

Cheddar Cheese Ball

1 8-ounce package cream cheese, softened
4 ounces sharp cheddar cheese, grated
1 tablespoon chopped pimiento
¼ teaspoon cayenne pepper
¼ teaspoon salt
1 tablespoon chopped green pepper
1 teaspoon chopped onion
1½ teaspoons Worcestershire sauce
    Walnuts, chopped

Put cream cheese into small mixing bowl; beat until smooth and creamy. Add remaining ingredients except walnuts. Blend well. Shape into a ball and roll in nuts. Chill thoroughly.

Blue Cheese Ball

1 8-ounce package cream cheese, softened
4 ounces blue cheese, crumbled
¼ cup chopped green onion
1 teaspoon lemon juice
1 clove garlic, minced
¼ teaspoon pepper
¼ teaspoon salt
½ cup chopped parsley

Combine all ingredients except parsley; blend well. Form mixture into a ball. Roll in parsley and chill thoroughly.

Salmon Ball

1 16-ounce can red salmon, drained
1 8-ounce package cream cheese, softened
1 small onion, finely chopped
2 tablespoons lemon juice
½ cup finely chopped parsley
¼ cup chopped nuts

Flake salmon into a bowl. Add cream cheese and blend well. Add onion and lemon juice; blend well. Shape into a ball and wrap in wax paper; refrigerate until firm. Sprinkle parsley and nuts on wax paper, mix well. Roll salmon ball in mix until coated. Keep refrigerated.

Spinach Spread

2 10-ounce packages frozen spinach, thawed and squeezed dry
3 tablespoons mayonnaise
3 tablespoons sour cream
¼ cup snipped green onions
1 6-ounce can water chestnuts, drained and chopped
1 teaspoon seasoned salt

Mix together all ingredients; chill. For a thinner consistency, add an additional tablespoon of mayonnaise and sour cream.

Photo Opposite
Blue Cheese Ball

THROUGH MY WINDOW

Pamela Kennedy

Friends for All Seasons

I was shopping not long ago in a large department store when an earnest clerk, spotting a potential customer, approached me, inquiring about my need for assistance.

"Just browsing," I replied.

"Well," she persisted, "perhaps if you could tell me what season you are, I could direct you to the appropriate section of our fashion department."

"Season?" I puzzled with a frown.

"Oh, don't you know your season, dear?" She clucked her tongue and shook her head slightly. "You see, everyone falls into a certain season depending upon her hair color, eye color, and skin tone. Our cosmetologist could help you discover what season you are. Then you'd know what colors to wear and you'd never have trouble shopping again!" She pointed toward the cosmetics department with a hopeful smile.

I started off in the suggested direction, but as soon as I was out of the clerk's line of sight, I veered left at the designer shoes and made a dash for the escalator. I really didn't care to have some stranger tell me what season she thought I belonged in. Besides, I had a suspicion I'd probably fall between seasons into some fashion "Twilight Zone" and never be able to wear anything but beige for the rest of my life!

How silly, I thought later, to pigeonhole people into seasons. And then I began to think of the women I know and cherish as friends. Only I wasn't thinking so much of their hair and their eyes as of their personalities and of the parts of themselves they gave to me, enriching my life so immeasurably. And it was funny how, as I thought of them, I could picture them as friends from different seasons.

There are some who sparkle with joy and radiate cheer like a sunny summer morning. Their optimism and enthusiasm are contagious, filling any room they enter. No one rains on their parade! Their conversations bubble over with encouragement and hope: "I knew you could do it!" "Don't let 'em get you down!" "Things are looking up!" I never remain in the doldrums with these summer people around.

And as I thought of autumn's warmth and color, of its homey scents and rich harvest, other people came to mind—friends from home, from years ago. And though we've changed and grown, our friendships remain. Their telephone calls and notes bring back shared memories, both sweet and sorrowful. These are friends who "knew me when." With them there is no need to impress or excuse. How great to bask in the autumnal warmth of these time-tested friendships.

I pictured the chill of winter, which drives me indoors to the fire when snow lies deep in the garden and soup simmers in the pot, and I was reminded of winter friends. These are the listeners, the thoughtful, pensive ones who share their wisdom as gently as the falling snow. They hear with their hearts and can wrap their understanding around me like a hug, dispelling the chill of self-doubt. What a wonderful thing to have dear winter friends!

But what of spring? Springtime people bring a freshness to life. They nudge and push me out of my ruts as insistently as a crocus pierces the cold earth. They identify and encourage hidden potential I never knew I had, daring me to try new things, accept new challenges, and cast off old habits. They make me change and grow—processes that aren't always easy but make me more mature, more insightful, more fulfilled. I'm thankful for my springtime friends who never allow me to become too comfortable or self-satisfied.

After giving it some thought, I've decided there might be something to this seasonal stuff after all. But I'm glad I'm not limited by a fashion designer's idea of the type of friend I need. I'm grateful that the Grand Designer who created me has blessed me with precious friends for *all* seasons.

Pamela Kennedy is a freelance writer of short stories, articles, essays, and children's books. Married to a naval officer and mother of three children, she has made her home on both U.S. coasts and currently resides in Hawaii. She draws her material from her own experiences and memories, adding bits of imagination to create a story or mood.

PRECIOUS GIFTS

M.B. Harrington

There are treasures to be hoarded,
Wealth that pays rich dividend;
But I find surpassing wonder
In the precious words "my friend."

Treasures fail to feed the hungry;
Wealth we rapidly can spend;
There are values more enduring
In the kindness of a friend.

Flowers fade and spring leaves wither;
Seasons come to birth and end.
Time in passing treats us kindly
When it leaves to us a friend.

God's good gifts are freely given,
And His thought we apprehend
When He speaks with true affection
Through the soft words of a friend.

Woman with a Cat; Auguste RENOIR; National Gallery of Art,
Washington; Gift of Mr. and Mrs. Benjamin E. Levy.

God's Gold

Dan A. Hoover

Sunny face of deepest summer,
Smiling countenance of gold
Waving over blooming garden,
Sturdy-stemmed, broad-leaved, and bold.

Whispering a rustling welcome
To each cool September dawn,
Dark green leaves as rough as leather
Follow sunshine until it's gone.

Grateful for each cooling raindrop,
Petals sip night's star-kissed dew;
Morning finds her decked with diamonds,
Sunray-brilliant, fresh, and new.

Golden beauty for beholders,
Nectar for the summer bee,
Seed store for sojourning songsters—
God's gold generosity.

FLOWER CALENDAR

Marian F. Daggett

The flowers of April
Are babies fair—
Pink cheeks, blue eyes,
And yellow hair.

The flowers of May
Are laughing flirts—
All wiles, gay smiles,
And gaudy skirts!

The flowers of June
Are lovely brides—
So pure, demure,
With blushing pride.

The flowers of summer
Are matrons neat—
Sturdy and starchy
Through all the heat.

The flowers of autumn
Haunt the heart—
Bright glow, brave show,
Dressed to depart.

CRAFTWORKS

Tokens of Friendship

The expression of friendship need not involve expensive gifts. Often the greatest happiness comes from a handmade token that reflects interests which only a friend can share. These easy-to-make gifts show how a little dab of color here and there can transform simple items into priceless treasures.

Decorated Baskets
Materials Needed:
Mushroom baskets (Ask the produce manager of your grocery store to save these for you.)
Aluminum foil for paint palette
Acrylic paint in red, green, yellow, royal blue, and orange
#3 and #5 paintbrushes for basket with painted flowers
Small sponge for sponge-print basket

Decorating Basket with Painted Flowers:

Using one color at a time, paint flowers all around the basket. Use both #3 and #5 brushes and all of the colors. When flowers have dried, paint green stems and leaves with #3 brush all around the basket to finish.

Decorating Sponge-Print Basket:

Pour one tablespoon of your first color of paint onto foil palette and dip the corner of your sponge into the paint. Dab paint gently all around the basket. Allow paint to dry before going on to the next color. Clean sponge well before changing colors.

Line finished baskets with brightly colored tissue paper, cloth, straw, or moss and fill with seed packets, plants, bulbs, garden books, garden gloves or whatever will make a very special gift for the garden lover.

Picture Frame

Any purchased acrylic picture frame can become a customized gift with a little effort. Enamel paint is recommended for a long-lasting, washable gift:

Materials Needed:
5-by-7-inch acrylic frame
Enamel paint in red, light blue, yellow, and green
#0 and #1 brushes
Paintbrush cleaner
White construction paper

Painting Frame:

Clean the frame with glass cleaner. Using the #1 brush, print FRIENDS FOREVER in red paint on the frame. Starting from the top right or left corner of the frame, paint blue forget-me-nots by making four dots to form a flower, using a #0 brush. When dry, make a yellow dot in the center of each flower, also with #0 brush. Paint green leaves randomly with #0 brush. Cut white construction paper to fit in the frame as a background for your favorite snapshot of you and your friend.

Joan Alberstadt

Joan Alberstadt is a former commercial artist who has always enjoyed sewing her children's clothes and making special gifts for her friends and family. The growing demand for her unique designs has resulted in her own business, the Cat's Meow, which she conducts from her home in Nashville, Tennessee.

Photo Opposite
Gerald Koser

Write a Letter

Craig E. Sathoff

When heart and mind traverse the years
To friends no longer near,
It's time to write a cheerful note
To let them know you care.

A letter is a special bond
For friends who are apart,
Who, separated by the miles,
Are very near in heart.

A bit of news, a touch of cheer,
A helpful hint or two
Will prove a treasured visitor
That pleases through and through.

A letter brings a twofold joy,
For he who reads the note
Is just as filled with friendship's gift
As was the one who wrote.

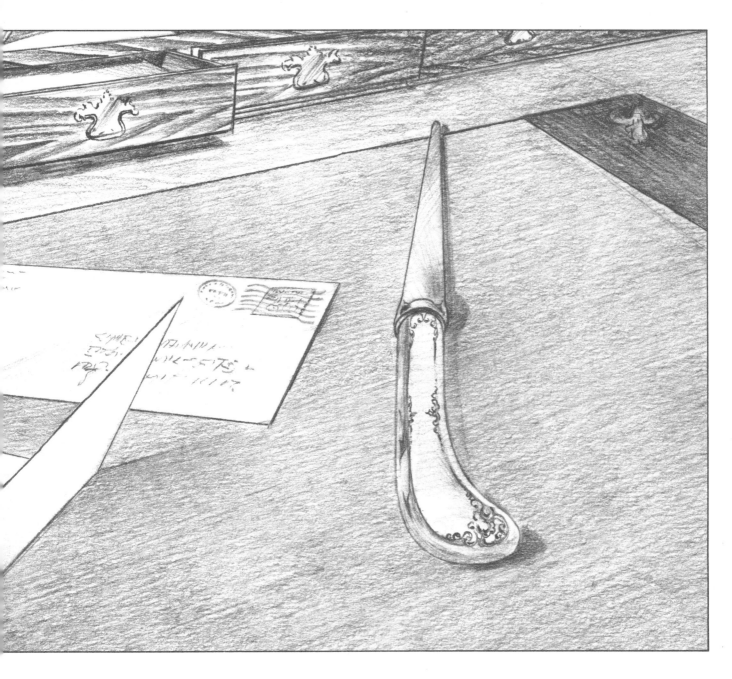

A Letter

Peggy Mlcuch

Isn't a letter a wonderful thing?
There's so very much it can do—
Your letters are just like a visit
Whenever I can't be with you.

Your letters are so very welcome—
I hurry each morning at ten,
Out to the mailbox down by the road
To see if we'll visit again.

Some letters bring tidings of gladness,
And some bring me news that you're blue;
Whatever the contents, I never can wait
To share those few moments with you.

Roadside Stand

Fred Toothaker

Along the highways out of town,
We find in much demand
A most convenient sight today,
The country roadside stand.

It's stocked with produce from the farm:
Potatoes, fruit, and such;
Sweet honeycombs to spread on bread
And apples cool to touch.

Travelers who pass this stand
On a cheerful autumn day
Find shelves of jellies and preserves
To carry on their way.

There's cabbage, rutabaga, and
Red radishes galore.
There's cottage cheese and eggs so fresh,
Just laid the day before.

Great hams, smoked and sugar cured,
Hang heavily for the taking,
While pumpkins canned and pumpkins whole
Shine, ready for pie making.

This time of thanks and harvest glows
At every roadside stand,
Where colorfully spread before us is
The bounty of the land.

Photo Opposite
COUNTRY STORE
SOUTH WOODSTOCK, VERMONT
Henry J. Hupp/Laatsch-Hupp Photo

A Slice of Life

Edgar A. Guest

ish wiping was a task that I avoided whenever I could. Oh, I used to do it willingly enough, but I had no great pride in it. After a little party at the home, when the last guest had departed, I lived in fear that she would say to me: "Come on, let's do the dishes before we go to bed," and I am sure there isn't a home in the land where, after an evening of friendship, that has not been said. I never thought I should want to hear that plea again, but it is so different now. I don't know just how to say it, but I think the happiest men in the land must be those who have wives who say to them: "Come on, let's do the dishes; it will only take a few minutes."

When the dinner party's over and the friends have said: "Good-bye"
There are ashtrays to be emptied which with weariness you eye.
There's a room or two to straighten ere you turn to climb the stairs,
And you mustn't leave the parlor filled with dinner-table chairs.
But the task that most I dreaded, following several hours of fun,
Was that stack of greasy dishes she insisted must be done.

"It's too late!" I used to mutter. "Wait till morning when I've gone."
"It will only take a minute," she would answer, "So come on!"
And she'd lead me to the kitchen. By the way she tossed her head,
Well, I knew I'd dry those dishes or I'd never get to bed.
So from kitchen to the cupboard I was kept upon the run,
Till she said: "I feel much better now we've got the dishes done."

Oh, I don't know how to write it, but today the way I think,
It would fill my soul with rapture to see dishes in the sink.
I'd give all I own this minute, after dinner we had planned,
Once again to stand beside her, taking saucers from her hand.
I'd wipe dishes night and morning till my time of life was through,
And I'd thank the Lord above me that the task was mine to do.

Edgar A. Guest began his illustrious career in 1895 at the age of fourteen when his work appeared in the Detroit Free Press. *His column was syndicated in over 300 newspapers, and he became known as "The Poet of the People." Mr. Guest captured the hearts of vast radio audiences with his weekly program, "It Can Be Done" and, until his death in 1959, published many treasured volumes of poetry.*

THE STRENGTH OF A FRIEND

Beverly J. Anderson

I stood one day at my wits end,
Then you came in the door, my friend;
And just your very presence brought
A ray of light for which I'd sought.
And as we sat and talked awhile,
My frown soon changed into a smile;
New hope sprang forth, dispelling fear;
The path ahead became more clear.
You truly seemed to understand—
Your spoken word, warm clasp of hand
Were what I needed that bleak day,
And I thank God you passed my way.
Now, unafraid, with courage strong,
I face each day with joyous song.
And if some day I see a friend
Who stands alone, at his wits end,
I'll pray that I to him will be
The caring friend you were to me.

32

Photo Opposite
THE OPENED GATE
H. Armstrong Roberts

Henry Ford and Thomas Edison: Friendship

Cynthia Wyatt

Imagine a beautiful September afternoon back in 1928 in Michigan. The air is crisp and clear, pearly white clouds move briskly across a clarion blue Michigan sky, and the trees are full of their green livelihood.

A small fleet of automobiles fills a dusty road-side pull-off and several men disembark at once. Four distinguished-looking gentlemen pause for a moment for a group photograph. Then, walking purposefully, they make their way along the wood's edge and sift silently into the tree line. They are all veterans of what have by now become famous hikes and camping trips, and theirs is a charmed circle indeed.

The leader of the group is a small wiry man who,

although in his sixties, still runs several miles each day and looks forward to camping trips with his friends with the glee of a ten-year-old boy. He is Henry Ford, and with him are his friends Harvey Firestone, whose company produces tires for Ford cars, and John Burroughs, the naturalist, author, and elder statesman of the group, whose long white beard and snowy white hair give him a soothsayer's countenance. The fourth man is the one for whom Ford has the most respect of all. He is Thomas Edison, the inventor who transformed American life.

Throughout his life, Henry Ford was a man of simple tastes and strong beliefs. He eschewed alcohol and tobacco and believed in the power of fresh air, exercise, and enlightened diet to prolong life. And Thomas Edison was his hero.

When Ford was still a young man, Edison was already famous for revolutionizing the telegraph industry for Western Union and establishing his own laboratory in Menlo Park, New Jersey. In effect, Edison introduced to the field of research the very thing which Ford was to later introduce to automobile production: the assembly line. The makeshift building in Menlo Park housed the first industrial research laboratory, staffed with machinists and clockmakers who had followed Edison when he left Western Union. When the laboratory was in full swing, Edison applied for over four hundred patents a year and invented the printing telegraph, the mimeograph, the carbon telephone transmitter, the microphone, the phonograph, the incandescent lamp, the alkaline storage battery, and the camera and film equipment for a budding new industry called "moving pictures." His work with telecommunications changed the meaning of the word *distance* forever, and his incandescent lamp reduced the power of the word *darkness* for all time.

From the moment they were introduced, theirs was a meeting of true minds. Both men aspired to improve the lives of common working people like their own humble forebears. And Edison spoke words of encouragement about the combustion-engine automobile to Ford, who was sixteen years his junior. Edison was to later comment that the automobile did "more to make America a nation of thinkers than any other invention." He wasn't talking about the Stanley Steamer, driven only by the well-to-do for recreation. He was talking about Ford's Model T, which was produced at a low cost and purchased by average working people all over the country.

Henry Ford was known to call history "bunk," but he decided that America must be shown its great heritage assembled in one fabulous display. He began collecting buildings within whose walls the shape of America had been decided and reassembled them in Dearborn, Michigan. His preference was for famous Americans who were largely self-taught, like himself. He moved the Wright brothers' bicycle shop from Dayton, Ohio; he appropriated a cabin which was (incorrectly) supposed to be Stephen Foster's birthplace; and he moved the workshop of the innovative botanist Luther Burbank from California. Ford clustered these with the homes and birthplaces of such famous Americans as Noah Webster and George Washington Carver.

But the kingpin of his village was the laboratory complex in Menlo Park where Edison and his staff made history. Ford had it moved along with an acre of New Jersey soil. He even hired workers to sift through the backyard trash heaps behind Edison's labs for artifacts of discovery and invention.

He was building what was to be the world's first theme park, and it eventually cost him thirty million dollars.

He called it the Edison Institute.

At the dedication of the Edison Institute on October 21, 1929, with President Hoover looking on, Ford staged a national demonstration of his friend's greatest accomplishment: electric light. Lights were extinguished all over the country, and when Edison threw a switch, they all came back on again. President Hoover brought Edison to the microphone to speak to the radio audience. It was reported that the old inventor wept. His speech ended with the words: "As to Henry Ford, words are inadequate to express my feelings. I can only say to you that, in the fullest and richest meaning of the term—he is my friend."

Thomas Edison died two years later. Henry Ford outlived him by another sixteen years, during which his most prized possession was a small glass vial containing Edison's last breath.

Today the Edison Institute is part of a 260-acre complex which includes Ford's personal collection of Americana as well as the Ford Museum. The Edison Institute is visited by millions of people annually. When visitors ask why Edison's Menlo Park laboratory is in Dearborn, Michigan, the answer is: it was brought there out of one man's desire to show it to the whole world. It was brought there out of one man's respect for all that had been accomplished within its walls.

It was brought there by one man's lifetime of feeling for another: friendship.

TRAVELER'S Diary

Michael McKeever

Photo Courtesy of Washington State Tourism Division · Washington State Ferry cruising the Puget Sound with Mt. Rainier in the background

How I Learned to Love Small Ferries

Some years ago I took my first conventional ferry ride. Which is to say I rode a ferry across a river. I was not impressed.

I grew up in the Pacific Northwest where the San Juan Islands lie like green emeralds scattered across the sea. And like most children of Puget Sound, I carry deeply rooted memories of the mighty Washington State ferries traversing miles of open sea, connecting the one hundred and seventy islands and the two thousand miles of coastline, carrying up to twelve hundred passengers and one hundred cars at a time. Virtually the lifeline of the island communities, the ferries can take three to four hours to get you to your destination, and if you pay attention, in the midst of all that beautiful scenery, you can actually spot killer whales off in the distance as you ride.

These ferries were named in the language of the northwest Indians, names with the sounds of potlatch drums in their heavy consonants. There is the silvery *Kalakala* and the *Tillikum* and huge superferries, part of British Columbia's service, like the *Hyak* and her sister, *Hiyu*.

For those of us in small towns and fishing villages, the ferries were our link to the big city of Seattle and the world beyond. They took young people away to college and the military and brought them safely home. Fast friendships were struck up on their decks, romances flowered, and a few babies were born.

36

By comparison, that homely little ferry which took me on a three-minute ride across some river somewhere years ago trudged wearily back and forth like one of Pharaoh's slaves hauling stone. At least it struck me so at the time, accustomed as I was to the grand scale of the Puget Sound fleet. But time has softened my arrogance, and my disdain has mellowed into affection. Small ferries have worked their charms on me. Wherever they are to be found across the country, they perform their job of linking isolated people with much more personality than any bridge ever could.

For example, who could not love the little ferry which carries commuters during the week and tourists on weekends across Virginia's Elizabeth River? Just over seventy feet long from stem to stern, she's a pint-sized version of a grand old Mississippi sternwheeler. From Norfolk to Portsmouth and back again, she steams along, paddle wheel flailing the water and smoke puffing from twin stacks.

Another memorable little ferry crosses the gilded waters of southern California's Balboa Bay, near Los Angeles, where the bay is edged by some of the most expensive real estate in America and sand is sold by the silver teaspoon. Luxury cars glisten in the sun while exquisite yachts gently tug at immaculate mooring lines.

The *Marietta*, San Diego Harbor Excursion fleet

But the Balboa Ferry is not a Sunday sailor, she's a tough flat-bottomed barge who works for a living. Faithful and uncomplaining, she makes the five-minute crossing, three cars to the load, dozens of times a day.

She's also one of the last bargains in America. Walk-aboard passengers pay a twenty-cent fare. Children pay only a dime. And there are precious few places left where you can buy a smile for a dime.

A world away from the plush precincts of Balboa Island is the gritty and remote Mexican border crossing at Los Ebanos, Texas. There the Los Ebanos Ferry crosses the muddy brown Rio Grande. Like the Balboa Ferry, it is a flat-bottomed barge that can carry up to three cars.

But the Los Ebanos Ferry is powered by the strength of her crew and is the last manually powered ferry in America. A stout steel cable strung across the hundred-yard-wide river and anchored to a strong ebony tree enables the crew, with straining muscles, to pull the ferry across the Rio Grande.

The *Silvergate* Ferryboat

The Old Ferry Landing, Coronado, California

A few tourists ride the Los Ebanos Ferry, but mostly her passengers are children on their way to school or local ranchers and farmers. Housewives cross over into Ciudad Diaz Ordaz, Mexico, for supplies. And on Sunday after services at the old La Lomita Mission, many people cross the river to be with friends and family.

Sunday is a time to relax, and even the hardworking men at the cable pause to tickle small children under the chin. Picnic baskets are opened and guitars brought forth. Soon music drifts across the Rio Grande, beloved songs in Spanish of loves won and lost, great heroes of the 1910 Revolution, and of life on the border.

Of course, transportation experts have long argued that bridges are more efficient than ferry service. Probably so; but they're not as much fun. Take, for example, the lesson learned in San Diego.

For decades San Diego had been served by a long, proud line of ferries with names like *Silver Strand* and *Ramona* and the little sidewheeler *Benicia*. Then, in 1969, San Diego proudly opened a soaring ribbon of steel and concrete connecting it with Coronado. With a new bridge spanning its bay, the city had no need for ferries. The engine rooms were silenced for what most thought would be the last time.

Some of San Diego's ferries went to good homes. The *Crown City* steamed out past Point Loma and turned northward. Now called the *Kulshan*, she plows

Puget Sound's chilly waters with the Washington State fleet.

Others were cut up for scrap. One old veteran was tied up in Los Angeles when a storm ripped her from the dock. They found her the next

The *Cabrillo*, San Diego Harbor Excursion fleet

The *Spirit of '76*, San Diego Harbor Excursion fleet

The *Monterray*, San Diego Harbor Excursion fleet

The Old Ferry Landing, Coronado, California

Photos Courtesy of San Diego Harbor Excursion

Dockside at The Old Ferry Landing

morning thrown up on the breakwater with a broken back.

Then, two years ago, a wonderful thing happened. The Star & Crescent boat *Silvergate* pulled out of her slip and began crossing the bay. After eighteen coldly efficient years, San Diego again has a ferry.

A little old lady of a boat, *Silvergate* has puttered up and down San Diego Bay since 1940. Today, brightened with new paint and festooned with passengers' bicycles, she tootles back and forth between San Diego and Coronado. Capitalizing on her background and personality, entrepreneurs have opened a speciality shopping center in Coronado called The Old Ferry Landing. It's hard to imagine as much charm in a shopping center named after a bridge.

Occasionally a haughty liner will slap her in the bow with its wake; but no matter, we who ride her love her. On some days up to three thousand of us

pass up the cheaper Coronado bridge for a ride on the *Silvergate*. It is well worth it.

I remember when I first surrendered to the magic of a small ferry.

It was early morning on Virginia's James River. The mist lay heavy on the water and the air was still. At Jamestown a replica of an English galleon rocked softly in the swells, flag limp at its mast.

The ferry wasn't much bigger than one of Ulysses Grant's gunboats. As she pulled away, reeds along the shore danced in her wake. She was no mighty *Hyak* with dolphins dancing in her froth; but I held my little daughter in my arms by the rail and was at peace.

Michael McKeever is a Contributing Editor of Country Inns *magazine and a frequent contributor to* Physicians Travel. *At journey's end, Michael enjoys returning home to Imperial Beach, California.*

COLLECTOR'S CORNER

Aladdin Lamps— "Magic" Since 1908

Vertique ribbed bowl and pedestal kerosene mantel lamps, 1937

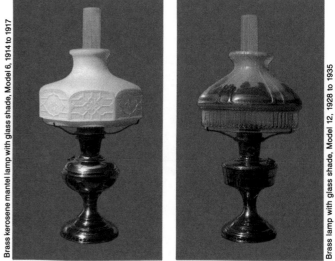

Brass kerosene mantel lamp with glass shade, Model 6, 1914 to 1917

Brass lamp with glass shade, Model 12, 1928 to 1935

Do you remember the pale yellow light of the coal-oil lamps? The smell as they sputtered and flickered? Smilin' Ed McConnell on the radio, telling you about the fabulous bright white light of the new Aladdin lamp? And when Aladdin lamps and shades brought color and style to rural America?

"The best rural home lamp in the world . . . Make your home bright and cheerful. . . . There is an Aladdin for every room in your home. . . . Be wise, Aladdinize and save your eyes." These early advertising claims tell the story of a need fulfilled. Smilin' Ed McConnell became "The Aladdin Lamp Man" as a well-known radio personality during the 1930s and 1940s. He touched the lives of millions of housewives through his hymns, stories, and humor. He said in one program: "Honey, a house without an Aladdin kerosene or electric lamp is like a house without a door. Incomplete!" Through his irresistible and personable style, he described the latest of Aladdin products and made everyone want to buy an Aladdin whether they had electricity or not.

The now-famous Aladdin lamps brought much-needed white, bright light to the farm homes beyond the electrical high line. Millions of people in rural America depended on the superior light of Aladdin lamps for more than half a century.

The Aladdin also furnished a beacon in many remote lighthouses and gave modern white light to forest rangers in isolated watchtowers and cabins. Trainmen on railroads did their clerical work by the light of the Aladdin caboose lamp. In times of power-crippling hurricanes and floods, the Aladdin brought steady light to hospital operating rooms and flood control centers.

The "secret" was the mantle which incandesced intense, pure white light and the tall chimney which drew in air for complete and efficient combustion of the coal-oil (also known as kerosene). Today Aladdin lamps continue to furnish dependable light in underdeveloped countries. They stand by, ready to come to our rescue during power failures, and are highly prized among collectors for use and display in their homes.

Seventeen successive lamp models have been developed in the past eighty years. The changes from model to model may not be obvious as some were subtle internal modifications to improve burning characteristics. However, others involved striking changes in the external design. All models except the first four are clearly marked "Aladdin" along with the model number (e.g., Model 11) on the wick-raising knob. Most of the early models (1-12) were made entirely of brass plated with a bright "silver-like" nickel finish.

Glass coal-oil lamps in a variety of colorful

styles were made from 1932 to 1955. The change to glass lamps lowered the costs so that more rural people could afford the superior light provided by an Aladdin. During the Depression years, an estimated six million farmhouses still depended on kerosene or gas for lighting. Also, glass permitted Aladdin to offer a wide range of attractive designs and colors for any room in the house. The many models, designs, and colors give today's collectors over a hundred different table lamps to research for their collections.

Table lamps accounted for the greatest number of sales; however, Aladdin also made hanging lamps, chandeliers, floor lamps, wall bracket lamps, and the already mentioned railroad caboose lamps which are still used today by some railroads.

Aladdin introduced their first line of electric lamps in 1930, and by the early 1940s, Aladdin clearly was established as one of America's leading manufacturers greatly due to the loyalty of hundreds of thousands of families who had been reared by the "magic" light of the kerosene Aladdin. As they did in the coal-oil era, the company continued to develop innovative designs. Their colorful paper shades, called Whip-o-lite, their famous ivory Alacite glass, and the lamps with night-lights were popular with home buyers. Well over one thousand different kinds of Aladdin electric lamps were made before sales were halted in 1956. Some cupids and nude figurine lamps that were considered risqué in their time are now highly sought by both Aladdin and art deco collectors.

My avocation has been to compile the history of and to collect Aladdin lamps. The "magic" of Aladdin has brought us many new friends through a newsletter that I publish for over a thousand collectors who "saw the light." We call ourselves "Aladdin Knights of the Mystic Light," a name taken from ceremonies the Aladdin company held over its sixty years of operation to give recognition to its distinguished employees. Our purpose is preservation of memorabilia of the kerosene and early electric era that was such an important part of rural America. As many collectors will tell you, purists use their electric lights only to find the match to light their kerosene Aladdins.

There is still an Aladdin lamp for every room of your home. Aladdin kerosene lamps are wonderful decorator lamps for today's country look as well as having real value when the power goes out. Check out the flea markets, your attic, or ask your grandmother—it is more than likely that you have an Aladdin at your fingertips that is just as useful, efficient, and attractive today as it was yesterday.

J.W. Courter

Opalique figurine lamp in the art deco style, *circa 1937*

Aladdin's Electric Vogue lamp, *circa 1932*

Many styles of Aladdin lamps, 1935 to 1948
Photography by J.W. Courter

J.W. Courter is the author of Aladdin—The Magic Name in Lamps *and* Aladdin Electric Lamps. *He is an Associate Professor of Horticulture at the University of Illinois and is the author of numerous publications in his agricultural specialty.*

Era Zistel

Most people praise a cat for catching a mouse but are indignant when the kill is a bird. Like the cat, I cannot make this fine distinction. To me (unlike the cat) both happenings are distressing, perhaps because I esteem mice as well as birds. However, this theory does not hold when applied to the shrew, a quarrelsome, gluttonous savage that is far from endearing; even so, I hold it in my hand with some sorrow for its demise. The fact is I cannot abide any killing, whether by the soldier on the battlefield, the hunter in the forest, or the cat in the garden.

Often I have chased after a cat of mine, uphill, downhill, in and out of brush, to discover what was in its mouth—most often the lowly shrew, inedible, but being warm and soft, somewhat more fun to play with than a paper ball. Having appropriated the catch, I do not punish the captor, not even when the prey turns out to be the much-loved thrush. Instead, we return to the house, and in exchange for what I have taken, I give a piece of meat. Not being covered with fur or feathers, this is preferred food, and in time the cat, eager to receive the reward, delivers to me immediately, without stopping to kill. I am given a bird, hold it in my hand for a moment, then open the hand and watch it fly away. Disposal of live wingless donations, however, is not that easy. The canny cat, observing the release, will try to make the catch all over again, to earn still more meat. That was why, for a while, I gave lodging to so many chipmunks.

The first two, acquired almost simultaneously, were Napper and Bricks, the latter so named because the first day, while I put together a cage, she was housed in a cardboard box labeled "No 465 Bricks." What kind of bricks they might have been was something I puzzled over briefly.

In those early days I didn't know that chipmunks would not live together amicably. Just to disprove the rule, these two did, sharing food and bed, at first nothing more than a heap of tissue on the floor of the cage, and working as a team to execute their many escapes. The cage had a small crack over the door, not big enough for anything but a worm to pass

through, I thought, but somehow the chipmunks got out, apparently by osmosis. I rebuilt the cage, giving it a tighter door. The chipmunks cased this new door and discovered it was locked with hooks. Thrusting their paws through the wire mesh, one fiddled with the top hook, the other with the bottom; soon both hooks were pushed up and the door open. I substituted hasps and bolts; they had the bolts out in no time. I tried large safety pins, and one chipmunk must have said to the other, "Elementary, my dear Watson." I had hardly turned my back before they had snapped open and removed the pins. Finally I produced a complicated lock that involved lengths of wire and washers that slid over the wire to fasten the door. After days and days of concentrated study and repeated endeavor, the chipmunks gave up trying to solve this puzzle, which sometimes baffled me also.

I like to give captive animals at least an approximation of the life they led when free. Chipmunks, I had learned, lived in burrows under rocks or roots of trees or, if they were shiftless, lazy, "tobacco road" members of the species, in crevices in stone walls or people's cellars. A properly enterprising chipmunk might have a veritable underground castle of many rooms; bed, storage, and bath. This castle, in keeping with its elegance, had to have several entrances, front, side, and service, so to speak. Once, trying to photograph a chipmunk in the wild, I was puzzled when she took the nut I offered and skittered it around and around my feet. After quite a while that must have greatly annoyed her, I discovered my foot was planted over her service entrance, through which the nut had to be taken, use of the front door for this purpose being highly improper.

To make Bricks and Napper feel at home, I spent much time and effort putting together wooden boxes that you could say were something like burrows. They chewed them up faster than I made them. I tried glass jars, which were indestructible, but eventually discarded because they tended to sweat. I bought sheet metal to make more boxes; they rusted and were difficult to clean. Finally our neighbor donated his empty tobacco tins, and the housing problem was solved. With small holes cut in for doorways, the cans were snug and dry, and I had only to remove the covers to clean them. . . .

. . . I had to clean out the chipmunks' houses, not because they were ever dirtied but because they got too full. Of all animals, these little ground squirrels are the most provident; even an empty stomach must stay that way while the larder is stocked. Bricks and Napper begged for nuts and more nuts, stuffed them in their storehouse until it overflowed, then put them in their sleeping quarters until there was no room left for sleeping and they had to spend the night curled up in a corner. At this stage I emptied the storehouse; over and over I gave them the same nuts, which didn't seem to bother them at all.

Usually I made my raids at night, when they were asleep; chipmunks have strong jaws and razor sharp teeth and tend to resent intrusion, even by the hand that feeds them. Once, after I had emptied the storehouse and put it back, suspicion or an untimely hunger woke Bricks. She went to what had been an overstocked larder, stood for a moment in the doorway of the empty can transfixed with disbelief, screamed, and scuttled back to wake Napper.

Together they went to confirm their loss, he somewhat groggily, his eyes only half open; they inspected the can, came out, looked around, went in again, and began to argue, quietly at first, then more and more heatedly, until they were trading curses and blows. Probably each accused the other of thievery.

The next morning they were friendly again but kept a wary eye on each other. Whenever one went into the storehouse, where a few nuts now rattled, the other followed to make sure the visit was legitimate.

From Gentle People *by Era Zistel, copyright © 1988. Published by J.N. Townsend Publishing, Exeter, New Hampshire. Used by permission of the publisher.*

Abou Ben Adhem

Leigh Hunt

Abou Ben Adhem (may his tribe increase!)
Awoke one night from a deep dream of peace
And saw within the moonlight in his room,
Making it rich, and like a lily in bloom,
An angel writing in a book of gold.
Exceeding peace had made Ben Adhem bold,
And to the Presence in the room he said,
"What writest thou?" The vision raised its head
And, with a look made all of sweet accord,
Answered, "The names of those who love the Lord."
"And is mine one?" said Abou. "Nay, not so,"
Replied the angel. Abou spoke more low,
But cheerily still, and said, "I pray thee, then,
Write me as one that loves his fellow men."

The angel wrote and vanished. The next night
It came again with a great wakening light
And showed the names whom love of God had blessed;
And lo! Ben Adhem's name led all the rest!

Photo Opposite
ASPEN TREES IN EARLY FALL
Dick Dietrich

BITS &

Labor Day

I am glad to see that a system of labor prevails in New England under which laborers can strike when they want to, where they are not obliged to work under all circumstances, and are not tied down and obliged to labor whether you pay them or not! I like the system which lets a man quit when he wants to, and wish it might prevail everywhere. One of the reasons why I am opposed to slavery is just here. What is the true condition of the laborer? I take it that it is best for all to leave each man free to acquire property as fast as he can. Some will get wealthy. I don't believe in a law to prevent a man from getting rich; it would do more harm than good. . . . When one starts poor, as most do in the face of life, free society is such that he knows he can better his condition. . . .

Abraham Lincoln

Endless Word

I know a word
That has no end:
Some call it love;
I call it *Friend*.

June Masters Bacher

Back to School

Let us make our education brave and preventive. Politics is an after-work, a poor patching. We are always a little late. The evil is done, the law is passed, and we begin the uphill agitation for repeal of that which we ought to have prevented. . . . We shall one day learn to supersede politics by education.

Ralph Waldo Emerson

America's future will be determined by the home and the school. The child becomes largely what it is taught; hence we must watch what we teach it, and how we live before it.

Jane Addams

Eighty percent of our criminals come from unsympathetic homes.

Hans Christian Andersen

FEELINGS

Every person's feelings have a front door and a side door by which they may be entered. The front door is on the street. Some keep it always open; some keep it latched; some locked; some bolted with a chain that will let you peep in but not get in; and some nail it up so that nothing can pass its threshold. This front door leads into a passage which opens into an anteroom and this into the interior apartments. The side door opens at once into the sacred chambers.

There is almost always at least one key to this side door. This is carried for years hidden in a mother's bosom. Fathers, brothers, sisters, and friends, often, but by no means so universally, have duplicates of it. The wedding ring conveys a right to one; alas, if none is given with it!

Oliver Wendell Holmes

46

PIECES

We are not sent into this world to do anything into which we cannot put our hearts. We have certain work to do for our bread, and that is to be done strenuously; other work to do for our delight, and that is to be done heartily; neither is to be done by halves and shifts, but with a will; and what is not worth this effort is not to be done at all. Perhaps all that we have to do is meant for nothing more than an exercise of the heart and of the will and is useless in itself; but, at all events, the little use it has may well be spared if it is not worth putting our hands and our strength to.

John Ruskin

Columbus Day

There's a bit of Columbus
    in every man's heart
As he looks at the lifetime
    he's wanting to chart:
A new way to his "Indies,"
    his personal shore
With its promise of riches
    for him to explore.

Perhaps it's a trade route
    no other has sought,
Or it might be a path
    undiscovered in thought—
Something still in the realm
    of the wholly ideal,
Waiting yet to be found—
    to be proven as real.

If this bit of Columbus
    were given a ship
Such as faith, hope, and courage
    can always equip,
Just imagine the continents
    people might find,
Sailing westward to lands
    of the heart and the mind!

Margaret Rorke

This I Pledge

If I could give you what I'd like today,
Only happiness I would bring,
Enough to last the whole year through.
I would make it sacred—some precious
thing—
Flawless, beautiful, everlasting.

But this we mortals cannot give;
So I pledge to you instead
A perpetual friendship, one that's true,
Strong enough to span all that lies ahead;
I will try to make it shine and keep it wisdom-fed.

Fannie Dee Robinette Pringle

When I Was Seventeen

Agnes Davenport Bond

When I was seventeen,
I taught a country school
Close by a stream
That broadened in a pool.

The rugged, branching oaks
Grew everywhere about
The old-time schoolhouse door,
Where youths ran in and out.

The benches in this school,
Where barefoot children learned,
Had room beneath to play
When teacher's back was turned.

A heavy cast-iron stove,
When needed, gave out heat;
A platform stood in front
With teacher's desk and seat.

I rang the clear-toned bell
When lessons should begin.
This was my usual call
To bring my children in.

It was a pleasant task
To fill a teacher's place,
And I remember yet
Each eager, happy face.

Those children now are grown
And scattered too, as well;
I might not know them now,
But I still have that bell.

They still would know its tone,
Though years have passed between
The days they brought me flowers
When I was seventeen.

48

Photo Opposite
1882 SUNNYVIEW SCHOOL
EAU CLAIRE, WISCONSIN
Barbara Laatsch Hupp/Laatsch-Hupp Photo

The One-Room Schoolhouse

Talbert A. Pond

The one-room schoolhouse was now a ramshackled piece of the past, with its roof and floor caving in with age and neglect and the schoolyard choked with weeds. As I stopped to gaze on the old relic, my mind was flooded with memories, as if ghosts of the past were floating out through the broken panes of glass and were taking possession of my mind.

I recalled the days of my youth at this school, and suddenly I remembered Percival McFaith, an old neighbor whose farm I passed each day as a boy, telling me that he had attended this school. His exact words were: "That's where I learned my three R's—Readin', Rightin', and 'Rithmetic."

From the stories related to me by Percival, I learned that most of the boys in his era only attended school for a few years before they went off to work for their families. Girls always had the opportunity to stay in school longer, although most never went past the eighth grade.

Times were hard then and supplies were short. The few books were shared, and most students used slate boards instead of the pens, pencils, and paper tablets that I took for granted. Blackboard and chalk were available, and one of the worst punishments was writing that thing which you wouldn't do ever again on the board a hundred or so times. The leather strap was saved for major punishments, and my hands had felt its bite many times, as had Percival's before me.

As I gazed in through the broken panes of glass, I noticed the corner in which you stood wearing a dunce cap when you came to school without your homework or acted the class clown.

The potbelly stove which still stood in the center of the room was covered with cobwebs. The oldest boy had the responsibility of being first to school in the morning to make sure that the fire was going by the time the teacher and the other students arrived. The room would be so cold that all the desks would be circled around the stove in the morning, only to be pushed to the far walls in the afternoon as the stove's production exceeded demand. I could almost smell the scorching odor of drying mittens or coats which had been placed too close to the stove.

The desks were still there and bore the carved initials of many generations. If turned over, I suspect that hidden wads of chewing gum would still be found on the bottom of almost every seat.

The trophy case in the far corner had been smashed by vandals, and the trophies for the most flowers brought in and for the most birds sighted by a student each year were missing. The flower trophy was the most prestigious because the flowers were seen by everyone, while the bird trophy was on the honor system. From the competition for these trophies grew the knowledge of and love for flowers and birds which I still have in my older age. Most students today would have difficulty distinguishing between a jack-in-the-pulpit and a cardinal.

My last glance inside the classroom was at the medicine cabinet on the back wall. I remember the many times that the teacher doubled as a nurse to patch up scratches and cuts acquired from climbing trees or from fistfights. The medicine cabinet also once contained a large brown bottle of cod-liver oil which the teacher administered each day by the tablespoonful, followed with a piece of orange to

kill the aftertaste. The students were overjoyed when the brown bottle was replaced with capsules which could be swallowed. Only the brave and the stupid bit into the capsules. With a bitter taste in my mouth, I turned from the window.

I walked to the cracked front steps of the school. The entryway where we hung our coats and left our overshoes was still standing. This entryway was the cause of my first strapping. We had a snowball fight outside, and one of the enemy ran to the entryway for protection. It was against the rules to throw snowballs into the entryway. The boy who was my intended victim kept sticking his head out, calling me names, and pulling his head back in. I saw movement, timed my throw, and let a snowball rip as hard as I could throw it. It landed with a loud *splat!* along the side of my teacher's head.

At the back of the school stood the two outhouses. The door on one was missing and the other's door hung by one hinge. The seats had been chewed by a family of porcupines looking for salt, and a pile of empty nutshells and seeds in the corner showed that it had become a feeding and storage area for a family of squirrels. The peeper knot was missing. For years the peeper knot had been carefully maintained by the boys. It gave a bird's-eye view from the boys' to the girls' outhouse, and for many was their first lesson in sex education.

Turning, I walked through a grove of old maples on my way back to the car. The huge tree trunks still showed the carved hearts and initials of long-forgotten loves. One tree in particular brought back fond memories to me.

When we drove by the school the next day, I pointed it out to my son. In the very words of Percival McFaith, I said, "That's where I learned my three R's—Readin', Rightin', and 'Rithmetic.'"

He turned, grinned, and said, "Dad, you should have spent more time on your English and diction."

51

That's What a Friend Is

P.K. Hallinan

A friend is a listener who'll always be there
When you've got a big secret you just have to share.
A friend is a sidekick who'll sit by your side
To make you feel better when you're troubled inside.

And when there's nothing to do on a wet rainy day,
A friend is a pal who'll come over to play.
Friends are just perfect for all kinds of things,
Like walking or talking or swinging on swings!

And for watching TV, a friend is the best
For cheering cartoons with and booing the rest
And then late at night, a friend is just right
For telling ghost stories when you've turned off the light.

Yes, a friend is the best one to hop, skip, or run with,
For playing some catch, or just having fun with.
You can sing and shout 'til your tonsils wear out,
'Cause that's what having a friend's all about!

What's a friend for? For all this and MUCH more!

A friend is a buddy who'll come to your aid
When he thinks you need help or you might be afraid.
A friend is a partner who'll stand back to back
To protect you from bullies or an Injun attack.

With a friend you can do what you most like to do!

You can have your own hideouts in dark, secret places
Or spend the whole day having caterpillar races
Or just drawing pictures of each other's faces.
You can laugh; you can cry; you can watch cars go by;
You can have a great time and not even try!
A friend is a person who likes to be there
'Cause you two make a wonderful pair!
And when all's said and done, the natural end is

A friend is a friend: THAT'S what a friend is!

Season Turnabout

Angela Gall

The final summer days unwind—
Feathered, petaled sights run out;
Crimson leafed ones to begin.
Neighborhood sounds, too, turn about;
Homes and streets now strangely still,
With summer's pandemonium spool
Of children, toys, and bikes unwound;
The noise and laughter back in school.

Indian Summer

S. Omar Barker

While daytime summer loafs and lingers,
Frost steals by night with chilly fingers
A bit of greenness from the hems
Of skirted meadows. Leafy stems
Of wild blue asters feel his pinch,
As gradually, inch by inch
And night by night, earth's verdure yields
To autumn hues on hills and fields.

This is the time of smoke-blue haze,
Bewitching Indian summer days,
When languid skies still dare to doubt
That summertime is bowing out.

The Fishermen

Fred Toothaker

Two barefoot boys with rolled up jeans
    and each with bamboo pole
Were headed down a country road
    with a fishing spot as their goal.
They'd planned this trip—those bosom pals—
    for days and weeks before,
And made up tackle they would use,
    not found in any store.

They'd filled an empty can with bait—
    the lure they hoped would strike
The fancy of a sucker or
    perhaps a baby pike.
They each had formed a vision of
    the string of fish they'd take,
And of how their moms would be so pleased
    with the meals that they could make.

To boys like these, and many more,
    the future's in their hands;
And they will furnish leadership
    As this great land demands.
Our world, we're sure, will always need
    to have such "fishermen"
Who, if their string of fish is short,
    will bait their hook again.

The Harvest of Rutherford Hardin

J. Landman Gay

Rutherford Hardin stood out in the garden
One fine autumn morn in October,
He gazed at the corn with a mixture of scorn
And regret that he could not get over.
He mused that the yard had been barren and hard,
His mem'ry of spring now residual.
He'd planted his seed with regard to the need
And requirement for each individual.

The raking and sowing, the weeding and hoeing
Took somewhat more time than he'd planned it.
The turnips got bugs and the strawberries slugs,
Though he'd sprayed as occasion demanded.

Sometime near mid-season the wasps and the bees and
The locusts decided to stop off.
The bees did no harm, but the locusts did swarm
And eventually carried his crop off.

The little remaining he'd hoped, by obtaining
Some netting, to save from denuding.
But worms crawled under to loot and to plunder,
And birds ate the tendrils protruding.
Distressed all the more, he'd declared all-out war
And had staked out his beagle to guard it,
Whose barking did nothing against the dread ergot,
And he and his corn were soon parted.

So now it was fall, and he surveyed his haul,
Withered strawberries looking like lug nuts,
A yellowed tomato, three beans, a potato,
With feelings approaching repugnance.
But bravely resigned in this thoughts, he opined
On the paltry result of his slaving,
And in consolation for this desolation
Said he, ''But the money I'm saving!''

We Played Together

Edna Jaques

"We played together"—what a lovely bond
That once you fished in quiet country streams
Or laid full-length upon the tawny grass
And told each shyly of your dreams.

"We played together"—in your boyhood years,
Learned the same lessons from the selfsame book,
Found quiet pathways in the scented woods,
Waded the golden shallows of a brook.

"We played together"—knew the selfsame joys,
Felt the same thrill of wonder at the sight
Of white sails bending as the ships went by
Down the long quiet highways of the night.

"We played together"—and though years divide,
No dearer bond in all a world of care
Can keep us closer to each other's heart
Than these old blessed memories that we share.

Photo Opposite
FRIENDS ARE PUDDLE WONDERFUL
Robert Cushman Hayes

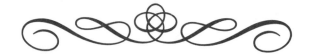

Father Thumps on the Floor

Clarence Day

Old Margaret was just the kind of cook that we wanted. Lots of cooks can do rich dishes well. Margaret couldn't. But she cooked simple, every-day dishes in a way that made our mouths water. Her apple pies were the most satisfying pies I've ever tasted. Her warmed-up potatoes were so delicious, I could have made my whole dinner of them.

Yet even Margaret sometimes miscalculated. A large, royal-looking steak would be set before Father, which, upon being cut into, would turn out to be too underdone. Father's face would darken with disappointment. If the earth had begun to wobble and reel in its orbit, he could scarcely have been more disapproving. He would raise his foot under the table and stamp slowly and heavily

three times on the rug. *Thud*; *thud*; *thud*.

At this solemn signal, we would hear Margaret leave the kitchen below us and come clumping step by step up the stairs to the dining-room door.

"Margaret, look at that steak."

Margaret would step nearer and peer with a shocked look at the platter. "The Lord bless us and save us," she would say to herself in a low voice. She would then seize the platter and make off with it to better it the best way she could, and Father would gloomily wait and eat a few vegetables and pour out a fresh glass of claret.

Father and Margaret were united by the intense interest they both took in cooking. Each understood the other instinctively. They had a complete fellow-feeling. Mother's great interest was in babies—she

had never been taught how to cook. All she wanted was to keep Father pleased somehow; and if it was too difficult, she didn't always care about even that.

At the table it was Father who carved the fowl or sliced the roast lamb or beef. I liked to watch him whet the knife and go at it. He had such a fine, easy hand. To a hungry boy, he seemed over-deliberate and exact in his strokes, yet in a moment or two he had done. And usually the cooking had been as superb as the carving. Sometimes it was so perfect that Father's face would crinkle with pleasure, and with a wink at us, he'd summon Margaret with his usual three measured thumps. She would appear, clutching her skirts with both hands and looking worried. "What's wanting?" she'd ask.

"Margaret," Father would tell her affectionately, "that fricasseed chicken is *good*."

Margaret would turn her wrinkled face aside and look down and push the flat of her hand out toward Father. It was the same gesture she used when she said "Get along with you" to flatterers. She couldn't say that to Father, but she would beam at him, and turn and go out, and stump back down the dark little stairs without ever a word.

Every once in a while, when the household bills were getting too high, a platter with three tiny French chops on it would be placed before Father, and a larger dish full of cold corned beef or Irish stew before Mother. At this sight we boys would stop talking and become round-eyed and still.

Father would look over at Mother's dish to see if it seemed appetizing, for he often said there was nothing better than one of Margaret's stews. The stew usually seemed possible enough to him, yet not quite what he wanted. He would then ask Mother if she'd have a chop.

Mother always said, "No."

"They look nice and juicy," Father would urge her, but she would say again she didn't want any and turn her eyes away from the platter.

Father would then look around at the rest of us, doubtfully. He had four sons, all with appetites. He would clear his throat as though getting ready to offer a chop to each boy in turn, but he usually compromised by saying, "Will anyone else have a chop?"

"No, Clare," Mother would quickly and impatiently reply, "they're for you. The rest of us are going to have stew tonight." And she'd smile brightly but a little watchfully around at us boys, to be sure that we were making no fuss about it, while she hurried to get the thing settled.

We boys would then earnestly watch Father while he ate the three chops.

Not that we didn't like Margaret's stew, which was the best in the world, but we regarded dinner as a special occasion, and we often had stew for lunch.

If some of us had taken up Father's offer and left him with only one chop or none, I suppose that he would have asked Mother, "Where are the rest of the chops?" and been very cross about it when she told him there weren't any more. But his offer of them to us was sincere, though it cost him a struggle. He wanted plenty of food bought for everyone. His instincts were generous. Only, it made him cross if he suffered for those generous instincts.

Long after Margaret died, Father was speaking one night of how good her things always had tasted.

"I wish she could hear you," said Mother. She smiled tenderly at the thought of that gallant and dear little figure. "If anybody ever was sure of going to heaven," she added, "I know it was Margaret."

This struck Father as a recommendation of the place. He took a sip of cognac and said casually, "I'll look her up when I get there. I'll have her take care of me."

Mother started to say something but checked herself.

"What's the matter?" he asked.

"Well, Clare dear," said Mother, "Margaret must be in some special part of heaven, she was so good. You'd be very fortunate, Clare, to get to the same part as Margaret."

"Hah!" Father said, suddenly scowling, "I'll make a devil of a row if I don't."

Half the Fun

Kathleen Y. Bergeron

Their yearly choice: ''What will I be?''
Then dress up, oh, so carefully,
Picking a bag that's big enough
To hold all of the tasty stuff.

They set off in the autumn breeze
Of dusk and never seem to freeze.
And though they do say ''Trick or Treat''
At every open door they meet,

I doubt they'd do a trick or care
If there was candy anywhere;
For when it's all been said and done,
It's ''going out'' that's half the fun.

October Thirty-First

Margaret Rorke

When we come to the end of October
And the gold has been spent in the leaves,
There's a sense in the air—sadly sober,
As though all of the atmosphere grieves.

In this pause there's a sort of suspension—
A sensation of hanging between—
Till earth yawns so's to soften the tension
And emits a most mystical scene.

Little witches and goblins come screeching
As they cast on the neighbors a spell—
With their bags and their breathless beseeching,
With the threat that we've come to know well.

In an hour or two it is ended.
Earth inhales with sigh drowsy, deep;
And October's no longer suspended.
Like the children, it's full and asleep.

64

Photo Opposite
HALLOWEEN
Dick Dietrich

The Week the War Began

After two weeks of the summer's hottest weather and a long drought, heavy thunderstorms in the northeastern U.S. cooled the air. In the South and the Far West, the sun shone brightly toward the end of a dry and pleasant summer in which the Dakotas reported first-rate wheat crops and Kansas cattle fattened faster than usual. . . .

Naturally, the "war of nerves" in Europe, hourly bulletins on which came over 40,800,000 radios, was the country's chief topic of conversation. Whether Franklin Roosevelt would run for a third term was a close runner-up. The old Greek theory that wars happen every thirty years because each generation is curious about the matter was subtly corroborated by the country's mood. John Dos Passos, Scott Fitzgerald, Cyril Hume, Sinclair Lewis, and most of the other good writers of the previous decade were either hacking in Hollywood or showing signs of being written out. Newcomers, with the possible exception of John Steinbeck in his *Grapes of Wrath*, did not seem to have much to say. . . .

Meanwhile, vacationists put away their fishing rods or put up their sailboats, examined their summer tans for the last time, and began thinking about moving back to the city. Over the long holiday weekend, at thousands of country clubs and roadhouses, the last dance music of the summer tinkled into the mild night. Much of it was "swing" or "boogie woogie" to which "cats" or "alligators" either danced the "shag" or listened in a proud, self-conscious trance. . . . Nine shows . . . had weathered New York's summer—among them: *Hellzapoppin, The Philadelphia Story, Yokel Boy, The Little Foxes,* and *Tobacco Road.* Meanwhile movies like *The Wizard of Oz*, with Jack Haley and Judy Garland, and *Fifth Avenue Girl*, starring Ginger Rogers, were packing the nation's biggest movie theatres. According to *Variety*, the most popular tune of the week was "Beer Barrel Polka," replacing "Three Little Fishies."

. . . John L. Lewis did not bother to answer the week's most sensational magazine article which charged that his Congress for Industrial Organizations was 1) shot through with Communism and 2) losing membership.

. . . Returning from Europe were Helen Hayes, Thomas J. Watson, Constance Bennett, Lee Shubert, Lilly Daché, and Norma Shearer, who explained her appearance on the grounds that it had seemed to her unfair to add to the responsibilities of a troubled continent that of watching out for Norma Shearer. Returning earlier than usual from shooting grouse in Scotland, J.P. Morgan explained that he had not noticed the fact that the *Queen Mary*'s lights were turned out early every night because he never stayed up late.

UPI/Bettmann Newsphotos

Mother and child arrive safely in New York after crossing the Atlantic as part of the largest passenger list in the history of the S.S. *Queen Mary.* Some 200 people slept on cots in public rooms. $44,550,000 in gold was on board and a constant guard was kept for enemy submarines.

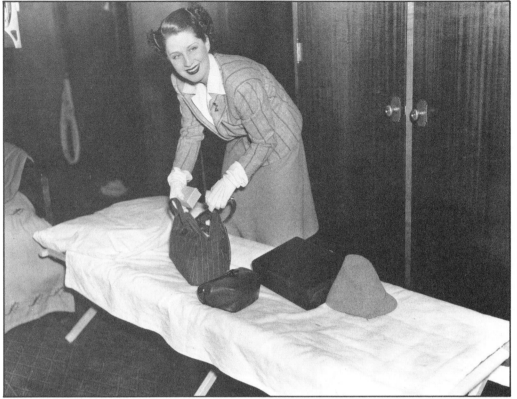

Movie star Norma Shearer making up her cot in the cabin she shared with three other women on the S.S. *Manhattan*, one of the cruise ships which evacuated hundreds of Americans from warring Europe in September, 1939. Every nook and cranny of the liner was occupied; even the grand salon was converted into a dormitory.

Henry Ford said there would be no war in Europe and that, if there were, the best thing would be for the rival armies "to blow up each other's munitions factories." Frank Buchman announced that "a hundred million people listening to God form a world opinion that will make war unnecessary."

. . . Dachshund lovers asked newspapers not to make dachshunds symbols of Germany. . . . Fannie Brice and Gracie Allen had a tricycle race at a Baby Snooks party. . . . Over the long Labor Day weekend, 22,000,000 cars drove 550,000,000 miles over U.S. roads. Nearly 200 people were killed and some 600 wounded in traffic accidents. Roughly $30,000,000 was spent on picnics, hot dogs, and gasoline. In the comic strips, Dick Tracy's ex-girl, Tess Trueheart, spent her days with a demented dog fancier. . . .

All this was activity which, in the U.S. last week, would have been no more noticeable than similar events in any other week save for the fact that they coincided with the start of another great European war. The word "another" was what made the start of the war at once more horrible and more unreal. If the first World War seemed incredible, the second seemed doubly so. . . .

Many things that were going on before the first World War continued to go on during it; and many things that started during the War continued to go on after it. There was, however, a deep change in the way that people experienced all things—a change expressed most simply by the fact that since 1914, "before the War" and "after the War" have been familiar phrases all over the world. When Europe went to war again last week, these phrases became suddenly meaningless. Like a grandfather's clock marking the hours, the guns in Poland and along the Rhine sounded a new interval of time in the century. Superficially, nothing in the U.S. changed much except the price of stock, the prices of food, the number of people who listened to the radios. Actually, everything was changed.

Whatever its effect upon the U.S. imagination, World War No. 2 seemed sure, like World War No. 1, to mark the end of an epoch. And the trivial aspects of that epoch—the sun over Kansas cattle, Dewey in Plattsburg, Good Humor trucks on the summer roads—acquired suddenly a strong importance. Against the background of war, they emerged sharp and impressive, like a conversation prolonged in the theatre after the rising of the curtain or like a familiar landscape made clear by lightning in the summer night.

Noel F. Busch

Life Magazine, September 18, 1939, © 1939 Time Inc. Reprinted by permission.

Drying Herbs

Gladys Taber

There are a number of ways to dry herbs, but we liked hanging them in the woodshed rather than drying them in the oven. Perhaps the best part is how good the house smells when you package them. Herb vinegars are easy and delicious. We brought the vinegar to a boil, dropped the herbs in, and bottled the infusion. The tarragon and dill are my favorites. Jill liked the mint vinegar with lamb, but I prefer melted currant jelly as a sauce.

The tarragon died out, and after several tries we gave it up. Possibly our winters were too cold. The sage spread and throve. So did the parsley. I like parsley in almost everything except pie. The borage has a delicate blue flower, nice to float on punch, and it is also pretty in bouquets. Jill never tried bay, but the herb shelf is never without it. I do not think a meat loaf amounts to much without bay leaves pressed in the top.

A pinch of rosemary glorifies green beans and is fine with sage in stuffings. Savory is good with beans and in salads, stews, and ragouts.

Herbs have been used medicinally for generations. William Coles, in *The Art of Simpling*, written in 1656, says: "There is no question that very wonderful effects may be wrought by Vertues which are enveloped within the compasse of the Green Mantles wherewith many Plants are adorned."

I do not know why herbs were called Simples—was it because they were, in early times, picked wild and were simple or natural to the land? Herb teas were called tisanes, and were made by pouring boiling water over the herb and steeping ten minutes. They cured almost anything if you understood them. Catnip tea, for instance, strengthened the kidneys; tansy tea was used for rheumatism; boneset was an emetic. When modern scientists found the foxglove contained digitalis, an important heart remedy, I suspect some long-gone herbwoman was saying, "Well, took you a long time to find that out."

Gladys Taber is the author of several humorous and wise books about Stillmeadow, the fine old country home to which Ms. Taber retreated from New York City with her longtime friend Jill and their young children. Stillmeadow had its share of bad plumbing, poor heating, and roof leaks, but the two friends persevered, raised their children, bred cocker spaniels, and enjoyed life to the fullest, as Ms. Taber's optimistic and good-hearted books reveal.

Photo Opposite
DRYING/POTTING ROOM AT HERB FARM
Grant Heilman Photography

The Old Armchair

Angela Gall

Bright sunlight streams into the room,
　　Each flickering, golden ray
A spotlight on the old armchair,
　　Problem of the day.

Moth-eaten, sunken from gross weight
　　Borne many blithesome years—
Should it retire with yesterday's
　　Fond memories and tears?

Although outmoded, it is loved
　　And sought by everyone;
Rough boys ride horses on worn arms;
　　Charles reads there in the sun.

At night it's Father's rendezvous,
　　Where smoke rings rise with cares;
I sit and sew in the fog of blue
　　And wish for more such chairs.

There worries mellow, blessings flow,
　　And "darning" is a pleasure.
Now is it strange I can't discard
　　The old armchair we treasure?

Old Treasures

Agnes Davenport Bond

I have a little table
Of rosewood, I am told,
Presented to my father
When he was three years old.

Its top is highly polished;
Its legs are deftly whorled;
And inlaid work of beauty
Along its side is curled.

I like that little table;
And too, I prize it more
Because it came from Boston
And cradles family lore.

I have another treasure
That I like, too, as well.
It has a task unceasing—
The time of day to tell.

It was my other father
Who gave me that old clock,
And daily I am hearing
Its musical tick-tock.

In Canada I often,
In that home so far away,
Admired that ancient timepiece
Which ticked on, night and day.

It stands now in a corner.
Erect and prim and high;
And the little Boston table
Is standing just close by.

What tales these two might tell me,
Tales of those olden times—
Perhaps the clock IS trying
to tell me with its chimes.

Wild Grapes

Edith Helstern

The grapes are ripe and the clusters glow
   like blue pearls in the golden light,
As the big gold moon of October
   roams the sky above at night.
Along the walls and fences,
   on swamp maples in lowlands too,
The colored fruit paints a picture
   in its prettiest color of blue.
Sometimes the long, trailing vines
   mass among sumac too,
Or cover the banks of brook or stream,
   spreading their wild grapes—blue.

In the bracing autumn days,
   the grapes are picked and used
In Mother's wild grape jelly,
   where their flavor is profuse.
The wildlife loves them too—
   the turkeys, pheasant, and grouse;
Bear, deer, opossum, and red fox
   will even come close to the house.
Sometimes in the fall, the waxwings,
   in flocks, congregate on a vine
And enjoy a meal of wild grapes
   just as we enjoy the sweet wine.

A walk on a quiet, sunlit road
   on a warm and mellow day—
You may savor the tangy-sweet fragrance
   of the grapes along the way.
The clusters shine among the foliage
   as their fragrance fills the air—
In a part of autumn's beauty
   that is boundless, everywhere.
And as we reap the harvest,
   we'll have autumn in a jar
On a long white day in winter—
   without reaching very far.

Deana Deck

Late Bloomer

When the treetops are ablaze with the oranges, yellows, and reds of fall, and gardens everywhere are giving themselves over entirely to the noisy

chrysanthemum, my senses begin to tire of the brilliance, and I long for the softer hues of spring and shade: the pinks, the pale blues, the soft lavender roses. Perhaps that's why the aster was put here—to bloom in August and September and lend a gentle wash of pastel to an otherwise flamboyant landscape.

If you live in an area of mild late winter, you can often include the frost-hardy aster in your Thanksgiving centerpiece. In colder regions they won't last quite so long, but they will still bring some variety of color to your late-season garden, and they shouldn't be overlooked.

Asters grow wild in many sections of the country. They are actually part of a large herb family and are easily grown, sturdy little plants. In their wild form, they tend to have a weedy appearance, but growers have been hard at work taming them, and today many attractive cultivars are available.

The New England aster (*Aster novae-angliae*), commonly known as the Michaelmas daisy, ranges in color from pink to mauve and purple, and at one and a half feet in height, usually does not require staking. This disease-free plant is one of the easiest to grow. Just give it sun and well-drained soil and divide every couple of years, and it will provide an abundance of feathery blossoms.

The New York aster (*A. novi-belgii*) is available in a wider variety of colors but is susceptible to powdery mildew and wilt; however, there are a number of new, disease-resistant varieties on the market. The New York aster is taller than the New England aster and usually looks better staked. (I avoid staking by simply clipping off branches as they begin to lean and putting them into vases.)

Several double-bloomed varieties are available. Colors include pure white, light and dark blue, and several shades of pink. In case you are still in the mood for bright color, you'll be glad to know there are also *novi-belgii* varieties that bloom in red and rich purple. The plant is also available in dwarf form for the front of the border.

Asters lend themselves well to arrangements, but they are equally interesting alone, standing in a sun-stained antique bottle on the breakfast table, or displayed in a bowl or small basket. Combined with a sprig of baby's breath, they are endearingly romantic.

One of the nice things about asters in the fall garden is that they provide one of the few touches of blue available at that time of the year. For years, in fact, I thought aster and blue were synonymous. That's because my early experience was limited to *A. frikartii*, a hybrid which ranges in color from pale blue to lavender, and which is one of the most popular of the garden asters. A tall variety, this old reliable summer-flowering aster is a good addition to the cutting garden because it blooms from June until the frost hits.

There is a popular annual *(Callistephus chinensis)* which is commonly called the garden aster even though it is not related to the true asters. Also known as the China aster, it produces a wide variety of colors—white, blue, pink, yellow, purple, lavender, and red. It ranges in form from an exceptionally dwarfed ground cover plant to a tall, strong-stemmed branching plant reaching three feet in height. The problem with this aster is that it is highly susceptible to aster yellows and fusarium wilt. Disease resistant varieties are available and should be sought after if you decide to add these to the garden.

The China aster is the only type that will not bloom again after being cut. For this reason it is a good idea to make successive plantings two weeks apart because these are exceptionally attractive in arrangements.

The true asters present no need for successive plantings. In fact, cutting them is actually good for the garden. The plant self-sows freely, but cultivars will not produce true to type; so if you don't cut the blooms, you will need to cut back faded blossoms to prevent seeds from forming.

Asters in the fall garden combine well with white and lavender chrysanthemums, and since both species require almost identical care and growing conditions, they do quite nicely planted side by side. They combine well in arrangements too, and their soft spring colors provide some refreshing variety in football season.

Deana Deck is a frequent contributor to Nashville *magazine, and her garden column is a regular feature in the* Tennessean. *Ms. Deck grows many types of asters in her cutting garden in Nashville, Tennessee.*

75

Country CHRONICLE
Lansing Christman

Walk in the soft September fields and listen to the sermons from the hills. God will speak to you through nature. There will be psalms in woodland and meadow, scriptures and songs in pasture and babbling brook. Now at summer's end, it is as if the creation of the world has been completed, and nature in its sabbath sings *hosannas* on high.

Walk in the September fields and they will hold out their arms and embrace you, friend to friend. The rush of the growing season is behind us. In this early autumn sun, sense the warmth and rhythm of life. Rest for a while on a lichened stone and tune your inner being to the glory of nature. The glory of early fall is that of accomplishment and satisfaction. Each golden September field wears the gentle glow of the mother who has seen her young fly on from the nest and become a part of this great world. Each combed September field shows the polished serenity of hard work rewarded.

The colors of September are the colors of glory.

Leaves of the hickories shine in their golden hues, and the reds of woodbine climb fence and tree. The earth is warmed by the scarlet of soft maples and sumac and the first feathery lemon-colored blooms of witch hazel on the ledge. The purples of the aster and the blazing flames of the goldenrod defy the hint of winter in the chilling evening breeze.

The fields are friendly and kind, and music can be heard from thicket and tree, from grass, and from running water near the glade. The meadowlark whistles as it takes flight from its fence-post perch. The air is pierced by the sharp *chrrring* of the woodchuck near its burrow on the farm's sidehill where it has been feeding on clover, preparing for its winter of sleep. Listen to the chipmunks and crickets, the bluebird's warble from an aging apple tree, the sweet refrain of the song sparrow from the alders down by the marsh.

Year-round, I go to the fields and listen. And God speaks to me through the wonder of His Creation. The fields befriend me anew each time I go to them for deep meditation. Yes, I am forever a friend to the fields.

The author of two published books, Lansing Christman has been contributing to Ideals *for almost twenty years. Mr. Christman has also been published in several American, foreign, and braille anthologies. He and his wife, Lucile, live in rural South Carolina where they enjoy the pleasures of the land around them.*

Readers' Forum

I greatly enjoy reading your books and always look forward to reading the next.

A. Michele Sexton
Englewood, Ohio

Your beautiful magazine has been in our home for many years, and I have always enjoyed and appreciated the beauty it contains and the thoughts expressed.

Leola G. Merrill
Farmington, Utah

Thank you for the beautiful reading material your subscription has provided me and my family with through the years.

Sonda Stepchuk
Romulus, Michigan

I look forward with joy when each issue of Ideals arrives in the mail. . . . My heart just wells over when I see how life is portrayed on the pages of your magazine. Keep up the wonderful work.

Frieda Kowert
Arcadia, California

I thoroughly enjoy every Ideals edition. Thank you for the kind of reading material the world needs. I have subscribed to Ideals for many years and have never been disappointed in its beauty and inspiration.

Helen Shick
New Bethlehem, Pennsylvania

God bless you. May you continue to publish a book that honors God, strengthens family ties and memories, and last but not least, just brings sheer pleasure and enjoyment to your readers.

Marie Schubert
College Park, Maryland

It is such a wonderful thing that at least one publishing corporation is endeavoring to uphold standards of beauty, decency, home and virtue and Godliness in our crazy, turbulent, declining world. Thanks!

Mrs. Flora Pencoff
Alexandra, Virginia

Back in 1964 we received Ideals as a gift subscription. . . . Our youngest son was five years old at the time and dearly loved this magazine. He would draw pictures from its pages for hours. I still have each and every one of those books and on February 28th that son will be thirty years old!

Mrs. Charles E. Wilkins
Port Clinton, Ohio

I have enjoyed Ideals since 1962—a beautiful book! I am so glad you have added the index and page numbers. Now we can tell others what page to look at for a poem when we use Ideals at our club meetings.

Ms. Clara Johnson
Mound City, South Dakota

* * *

Want to share your crafts and recipes?
Readers are invited to submit original craft ideas and original recipes for possible development and publication in future *Ideals* issues. Please send recipes or query letters for craft ideas (with photograph, if possible) to Editorial Features Department, Ideals Publishing Corporation, P.O. Box 140300, Nashville, Tennessee 37214-0300. Please do not send craft samples; they cannot be returned.

ideals
Celebrating Life's Most Treasured Moments

Photo Opposite
RED EAGLE POND
CONWAY, NEW HAMPSHIRE
Fred Sieb Photography